KOMODO
VACATION GUIDE
2023

The Essential and Ultimate Guide to Komodo's

Hotels, Cuisines, Shopping Tips, Insider's Tips,

Top Attractions, History, and Culture

ALFRED FLORES

Copyright © 2023, Alfred Flores

TABLE OF CONTENTS

INTRODUCTION

Step into a world of breathtaking beauty, untamed wilderness, and captivating adventures as you embark on a journey through the enchanting realm of Komodo. Nestled in the heart of the Indonesian archipelago, Komodo offers a symphony of natural wonders that will leave you spellbound and eager to explore its diverse landscapes, unique wildlife, and rich cultural tapestry.

Why Visit Komodo?

Unveil the allure of Komodo, where ancient legends meet modern-day wonder. This guide invites you to delve into an extraordinary destination that seamlessly blends rugged landscapes with serene beaches, ancient traditions with contemporary hospitality. Whether you're a nature enthusiast, an intrepid explorer, or a seeker of relaxation, Komodo promises an unforgettable escape that caters to every traveler's desire. Witness the iconic Komodo dragons in their untamed habitat, dive into vibrant coral reefs teeming with marine life, hike through lush jungles, or simply bask in the sun's golden embrace on pristine shores. The reasons to visit Komodo are as diverse as the experiences it offers.

How to Use This Guide

In your hands, you hold a comprehensive compass to navigate the wonders of Komodo. This guide has been meticulously curated to serve as your trusted companion, providing you with invaluable insights, practical tips, and insider recommendations to make the most of your vacation. Whether you're a first-time visitor or a returning explorer, you'll find detailed itineraries, local secrets, and everything in between to craft your perfect Komodo experience.

Komodo: Quick Facts and Statistics

Before you set foot on this extraordinary island, let's acquaint you with some essential facts and figures about Komodo:

- **Location:** Indonesian archipelago, situated between the islands of Flores and Sumbawa.
- **Time Zone:** Komodo Standard Time (KST), UTC+8.
- **Size:** Approximately 390 square kilometers.
- **Population:** Around 2,000 residents, predominantly from the Komodo ethnic group.

- **Language:** Bahasa Indonesia is the official language, while locals often speak the Komodo language.

- **Currency:** Indonesian Rupiah (IDR).

- **Climate:** Tropical climate with wet and dry seasons. The best time to visit is from April to June and September to November.

As you turn the pages of this guide, prepare to embark on an adventure that promises to awaken your senses and rejuvenate your spirit. Komodo awaits, ready to captivate you with its wonders and provide memories to last a lifetime. Let's begin this journey together, where discovery and delight go hand in hand.

CHAPTER ONE:
Discovering Komodo

Nestled among the vast Indonesian archipelago, Komodo is a mesmerizing jewel that attracts visitors from all over the world to see its extraordinary landscapes, meet its fabled residents, and immerse themselves in its rich history and culture. We explore Komodo's geographical insights, climate and weather patterns, historical significance, and the rich tapestry of cultural diversity that has woven the fabric of this unique place as we set out on our adventure of discovery through it.

Geographical Insights

Komodo, situated between the islands of Flores and Sumbawa, offers a breathtaking tableau of natural wonders. Its rugged terrain, characterized by undulating hills, dramatic cliffs, and pristine beaches, is a testament to the forces of nature that have shaped this land over millennia. The allure of Komodo is further heightened by its diverse ecosystems, ranging from lush rainforests teeming with flora and fauna to vibrant coral reefs that paint the underwater world with a kaleidoscope of colors.

The Komodo dragon, the region's namesake, is what makes Komodo so alluring. The Komodo National Park's rough terrain is home to these ancient reptiles, which are the biggest lizards on Earth. The park's status as a UNESCO World Heritage Site guarantees the preservation of this distinctive ecosystem, where these famous animals roam freely and provide an incredible window into a bygone past.

Climate and Weather

As diverse as Komodo's landscapes are, so is its climate. The island has a tropical climate with distinct wet and dry seasons, each of which contributes in a different way to the natural beauty of the island. From November through March, the rainy season, which delivers life-giving rainfall, renews the vegetation and creates a lush, colorful backdrop. The island is drenched in green during this season, and waterfalls pour down the slopes in a symphony of the glory of nature.

In contrast, the dry season, which lasts from April to October, gives the environment a warm tint and provides the best circumstances for both land and marine exploration. Divers and snorkelers can discover an underwater world teeming with marine life in the clean seas that surround Komodo. During this time, the beaches, which are bordered by blue waters, welcome visitors to take advantage of the coast's peace and quiet while they bask in the golden embrace of the sun.

Historical Significance

Beyond its natural splendor, Komodo is steeped in a rich tapestry of history that traces back centuries. The island's story is intertwined with the narratives of explorers, traders, and indigenous communities, each leaving an indelible mark on its cultural landscape.

The ancient Komodo dragon, a creature that has captivated people's imagination for decades, calls Komodo home, which serves as an example of its historical importance. These creatures have a timeless aura thanks to local history and stories, which has turned the island into a place of mystery and intrigue.

Cultural Diversity

The seamless fusion of tradition and contemporary in Komodo's cultural mosaic reflects the island's turbulent past. These environments have supported the Komodo ethnic group, from which the island gets its name, for many years. Their manner of life, which still has a strong connection to nature, shows how connected they are to the land and its inhabitants.

A kind and welcoming people ready to share its traditions, tales, and vivid customs welcomes travelers as they travel throughout Komodo. Festivals, dances, and rituals give an immersive experience that encourages a deeper understanding of the island's character and open a window into the core of Komodo's cultural legacy.

In conclusion, discovering Komodo is a multi-faceted journey that unveils a realm of unparalleled beauty, historical significance, and cultural diversity. From the majestic Komodo dragons to the lush landscapes and captivating traditions, each facet of this island's tapestry contributes to an experience that is both enriching and transformative. As we venture deeper into the heart of Komodo, we invite you to immerse yourself in its wonders, embrace its history, and connect with its people—a voyage of exploration that promises to leave an indelible mark on your soul.

CHAPTER TWO:
Planning Your Komodo Trip

An extraordinary trip filled with natural marvels, cultural experiences, and the thrill of exploration awaits those who set out on a visit to Komodo. It's crucial to empower yourself with practical knowledge as you prepare for your journey to this alluring location in order to guarantee a smooth and rewarding encounter. This guide will lead you through the complex logistics of organizing your Komodo journey, from picking the best time to come and comprehending admission procedures to booking lodging and transportation and protecting your vacation with travel insurance.

Best Time to Visit

The timing of your visit to Komodo can significantly influence the quality of your experience. The island experiences a tropical climate characterized by wet and dry seasons.

Generally, the dry season which runs from April to October, is the greatest time to travel. These are the best months for outdoor pursuits like hiking, diving, and beach outings because the weather is generally dry and pleasant. The waters are quiet and transparent, making them ideal for exploring underwater, while the natural surroundings make a beautiful backdrop for your travels.

The wet season, from November to March, brings occasional heavy rainfall and increased humidity. While this period may deter some travelers, it offers its own unique charm. The rains rejuvenate the flora, creating lush green landscapes, and waterfalls come alive in their full splendor. Additionally, the wet season is considered the best time for bird watching, as many species are more active during this time.

Visa and Entry Requirements

Before setting out on your Komodo adventure, ensure you have the necessary visas and meet the entry requirements for Indonesia. Visitors from many countries can obtain a tourist visa upon arrival, allowing for a stay of up to 30 days. However, these regulations can change, so it's essential to check with the Indonesian embassy or consulate in your home country for the latest information.

It's wise to apply for the necessary visa before your trip if you want to stay for an extended period of time or for a specified reason, such as job or study. Remember to check that your passport is valid for at least six months after the day you intend to leave Indonesia.

Getting to Komodo

Reaching the shores of Komodo involves a combination of air and sea travel. The starting point for most travelers is Ngurah Rai International Airport (Denpasar Airport) on the island of Bali, which serves as a major international gateway to Indonesia.

From Bali, you can take a domestic flight to Labuan Bajo, the main gateway to Komodo. Labuan Bajo's Komodo Airport is well-connected to Bali, Jakarta, and other major Indonesian cities. Flight availability may vary, so it's advisable to book your tickets in advance, especially during peak travel seasons.

Getting Around

Once you've landed in Labuan Bajo, you can get about Komodo and the area around it using a variety of transportation methods. Renting a car or scooter gives you the freedom to tour the island at your own speed. Make careful to follow local traffic laws and to have an international driving license.

Local transportation includes "ojeks" (motorcycle taxis) and "bemos" (small public vans), which are cost-effective ways to travel short distances. For island-hopping and visiting neighboring islands, organized tours and boat charters are popular choices, allowing you to experience the region's stunning marine beauty.

Accommodation Options

Komodo provides a wide variety of lodging choices to fit any traveler's needs and budget. The main hub, Labuan Bajo, offers a selection of hotels, guesthouses, and resorts that range in price from inexpensive to luxurious. Numerous of these places provide breathtaking ocean views and convenient harbor access for island excursions.

Consider staying in eco-friendly lodges or bungalows tucked away in the luxuriant vegetation for a more immersive experience. These choices enable you to interact with nature while causing the least amount of environmental damage possible.

Travel Insurance

Travel insurance is an essential part of organizing any vacation since it provides financial security and peace of mind in the event that unforeseen situations occur. Your travel insurance should provide coverage for misplaced luggage, medical emergencies, trip cancellations, or disruptions. To make sure your policy meets your needs and the activities you intend to participate in during your Komodo trip, it is advisable to thoroughly study the terms and coverage of your policy.

In order to ensure a seamless and rewarding trip, careful planning is necessary for your Komodo excursion. You'll be ready to set out on a voyage that promises to be a seamless fusion of exploration, leisure, and cultural immersion by picking the best time to visit, comprehending visa needs, organizing transportation, choosing accommodations, and obtaining travel insurance. This thorough planning will open the door for experiences that will last a lifetime as you explore the breathtaking scenery and rich culture of Komodo.

CHAPTER THREE:
Unveiling Komodo's Natural Wonders

Komodo, a realm of untouched beauty and breathtaking landscapes, stands as a testament to the splendor of nature's artistry. From the awe-inspiring Komodo National Park to the legendary dragons that roam its rugged terrains, the pristine beaches, vibrant coral reefs, and hidden lagoons that embellish its shores, and the underwater wonderland that awaits divers and snorkelers, Komodo's natural wonders are a symphony of marvels that invite travelers to immerse themselves in a world of discovery and wonder.

Komodo National Park

The Komodo National Park, a UNESCO World Heritage Site that spans a captivating archipelago, is at the center of the natural allure of Komodo. The park, which includes the islets Komodo, Rinca, and Padar, is a haven for biodiversity and a site of evolution. Savannas, mangroves, woodlands, and coral reefs are just a few of the various ecosystems in the park that support a staggering variety of plant and animal species.

Komodo Dragons and Wildlife

The Komodo dragon, or Varanus komodoensis, is the biggest living lizard and a well-known resident of the Komodo National Park. These extinct reptiles, frequently referred to as "living fossils," inspire respect and intrigue. Few people ever forget the experience of seeing these creatures in their native habitat, with their ancient aspect and imposing presence.

In addition to the dragons, the park is home to a staggering variety of species. The richness of Komodo National Park, which includes everything from deer and wild boars to rare bird species and marine life, is a living example of the delicate balance that nature maintains.

Pristine Beaches and Coral Reefs

The beaches along Komodo's coastline are pristine and almost otherworldly in appearance. A color-filled dance between the gentle beaches and the clear seas calms the spirit and encourages rest. The name Pink Beach refers to the beach's distinctive pink sands, which serve as a symbol of the island's allure. Visitors can enjoy the warmth of the sun, swim in the clear seas, and take in the striking contrast between the cerulean sea and the pastel shoreline.

Spectacular Diving and Snorkeling Sites

A magical realm awaits exploration beneath the surface of the nearby waterways. Both divers and snorkelers will find paradise in Komodo's underwater world. The coral reefs that grow here are some of the most colorful and diversified on the planet, supporting an array of aquatic species. Divers and snorkelers can spot rare pygmy seahorses that live in the reefs, manta rays that glide gracefully through the currents, bright coral formations crowded with fish, and more.

Caves and Hidden Lagoons

Beyond its terrestrial and marine environments, Komodo's natural wonders venture into the world of mystery and exploration. Secret lagoons and hidden caves dot the island, adding to the sensation of exploration. Gua Rangko, a secret cave pool with crystalline waters and ethereal sunlight, provides a special chance to swim in nature's private haven. These geological wonders offer relief from the tropical heat while also showcasing the artistic creations of nature in the forms and reflections that embellish their interiors.

Finally, exploring Komodo's natural beauties is an adventure into a world of amazing diversity and beauty. Komodo beckons with a symphony of natural wonders that grab the imagination and create a profound connection with the planet's complicated ecosystems, from the majestic Komodo dragons to the alluring coral reefs and the hidden riches that await in caves and lagoons. You'll find yourself in awe and astonishment as you travel the sceneries and plunge into the pristine waters, indelibly marked with the magnificence of Komodo's natural inheritance.

CHAPTER FOUR:
Exploring Komodo's Top Attractions

Komodo, a realm of untamed beauty and natural wonders, beckons adventurers to uncover its most captivating treasures. From the iconic Padar Island and the mesmerizing Pink Beach to the legendary Rinca Island and the serene oasis of Kanawa Island, and the panoramic vistas of Gili Lawa Darat, Komodo's top attractions promise an unforgettable journey of exploration and discovery. Join us as we venture into the heart of these remarkable destinations, each offering a unique glimpse into the diverse tapestry of Komodo's landscapes and experiences.

Padar Island

An island that appears to be a collage of scenery from all parts of the world, Padar Island is a tribute to nature's beauty. The viewpoint that rewards intrepid hikers with one of the most spectacular landscapes imaginable is the highlight of Padar Island. In a kaleidoscope of hues ranging from the deep greens of the forests to the brilliant blues of the surrounding seas, the steep hills, powdery beaches, and pristine bays of the island's top reveal a strange landscape with a short climb to its summit.

As the sun sets over Padar Island, the scenery becomes a work of art of silhouettes and shadows, illuminating the land and water with an ethereal glow. It's a scene that sticks in the mind and is proof of how awe- and wonder-inspiring the island is.

Pink Beach

Pink Beach, an enchanting stretch of shoreline, derives its name from the delicate hue of its sands, a rare and captivating phenomenon created by the interplay of red coral fragments and white sand. The result is a pastel paradise that exudes serenity and romance. Visitors to Pink Beach are greeted by a symphony of colors—the soft pink sands juxtaposed against the turquoise waters create a scene straight out of a dream.

Pink Beach offers a sensory experience that sparks the imagination and transports you to a world of natural harmony, whether you're taking a leisurely dip, snorkeling in the coral-rich seas, or simply enjoying the quiet ambiance.

Rinca Island

Rinca Island, a sister to Komodo Island, is renowned for its vibrant population of Komodo dragons and offers a unique opportunity to observe these majestic creatures in their natural habitat. As you embark on a guided trek through the island's landscapes, keep your senses heightened in anticipation of encountering these ancient reptiles.

With its intimidating presence and allure from prehistoric times, seeing a Komodo dragon is an experience that makes you more aware of the delicate balance of life in Komodo National Park. The guided excursions also provide you an understanding of the island's varied ecosystems and give you the chance to see a wide range of species, including deer, wild boars, and unusual birds.

Kanawa Island

In the Komodo archipelago, Kanawa Island is a quiet haven for visitors seeking peace and leisure. The pure white sands and crystal clear waters of this little, picture-perfect island provide a getaway from the hustle and bustle of daily life.

Around Kanawa Island, snorkeling displays a lively underwater environment teeming with marine life and colorful coral formations. The island's relaxed vibe and unspoiled environs make it the ideal place to go for leisurely strolls, sunbathing, and simply taking in nature's splendor.

Gili Lawa Darat

With its expansive vistas and dramatic landscapes, Gili Lawa Darat, a peak of natural grandeur, attracts both adventurers and photographers. Awe-inspiring views of Komodo's untamed beauty are the reward for the climb to Gili Lawa Darat's summit, which is accessible only by foot.

From here, one may take in the expansive vistas, the turquoise embrace of the surroundings, and the alluring curve of the nearby islands. Gili Lawa Darat transforms into a realm of golden tones as the sun sets, weaving a spell that leaves a permanent impact on the soul.

In conclusion, visiting Komodo's finest sights is a discovery voyage that reveals the island's astounding diversity and natural beauty. Each location offers a distinctive perspective on Komodo's beautiful landscapes and the wonders that inhabit them, from the panoramic paradise of Padar Island to the pastel sands of Pink Beach, the dragon kingdom on Rinca Island, the serene haven of Kanawa Island, and the breathtaking vistas of Gili Lawa Darat. You'll become engrossed in a tapestry of sensations as you travel through these unique locations, experiences that arouse awe, spark the imagination, and leave a lasting impression on your soul.

CHAPTER FIVE:
Komodo's Underwater Paradise

Beneath the sparkling surface of the cerulean waters surrounding Komodo lies a mesmerizing world of unparalleled beauty and biodiversity—a realm that beckons explorers and water enthusiasts to delve into its depths and uncover the secrets of Komodo's underwater paradise. From the intricate tapestry of marine life to the awe-inspiring dive sites and snorkeling adventures that await, and the steadfast conservation efforts that protect this fragile ecosystem, Komodo's underwater realm is a testament to the wonders of the natural world and the importance of preserving it for generations to come.

Marine Biodiversity

The aquatic biodiversity of Komodo is a symphony of hues, shapes, and actions that reflects the complex dance of life itself. The Komodo National Park's surrounding waters are home to a dizzying array of marine life, from tiny nudibranchs to enormous marine animals.

Coral reefs, frequently referred to as the ocean's rainforests, are a vital component of this thriving ecosystem. Numerous fish species, crustacean species, and mollusk species all use these reefs as homes, nurseries, and feeding places for their young. With their vivid colors and unique patterns, the coral formations add to the breathtaking backdrop they create.

Diving Excursions and Dive Sites

Komodo provides a portal to a world of up-close encounters with marine life for experienced divers. Numerous dive locations dot the waters, each having a distinct personality and charms of their own. Divers can swim among schools of fish, manta rays, and sharks at Batu Bolong, which is known for its cliff-like walls and a wealth of marine life. Underwater pinnacle Crystal Rock, which is teeming with brilliant corals, makes for a colorful setting for underwater photography.

As divers drift with the ocean currents and take in a dynamic view of marine life, the Blue Dragon drift dive promises to be an unforgettable experience. Komodo's diving sites accommodate divers of all levels and provide everything from thrilling drift dives to macro photography, making it a must-visit location for those looking to discover the secrets of the deep.

Snorkeling Adventures

Snorkeling offers an affordable and enthralling alternative to diving for those who want to experience Komodo's underwater world. Divers can observe the delicate ballet of fish darting in and out of coral formations, skim the surface of brilliant coral gardens, and gaze into deep caverns where marine life hides out.

Under the waters, where coral reefs flourish and marine life is abundant, the appropriately called Pink Beach gives snorkelers a kaleidoscope of colors. Snorkelers may get up close and personal with Komodo's marine biodiversity while using only a few pieces of equipment and a sense of awe.

Conservation Efforts

The allure of Komodo's underwater paradise is not without its challenges. As tourism and human activity increase, the delicate balance of this marine ecosystem becomes ever more fragile. Recognizing the importance of safeguarding this treasure trove of biodiversity, conservation efforts have taken center stage.

Protecting coral reefs, reducing human impact, and educating people and visitors about sustainable practices are the main goals of local projects, which are supported by cooperation from governmental agencies and international organizations. To make sure that interactions with marine life do not upset or injure these delicate species, responsible diving and snorkeling standards are advocated.

The underwater paradise of Komodo is a place of wonder and amazement, a haven where ecosystems coexist in complex harmony and marine life thrives. Komodo's underwater environment offers a view into the wonder of the natural world, from the wide variety of animals that live on coral reefs to the exhilaration of diving into the unknown and the peace of snorkeling along the surface.

But with this beauty comes a duty to safeguard and preserve. Let's be considerate of our influence as we explore the depths and marvel at the wonders of this underwater world and help with conservation efforts to keep these waters brimming with life for future generations. We become guardians of Komodo's underwater paradise by embracing sustainable practices and supporting programs that protect this vulnerable ecosystem, ensuring that its beauty endures for all time.

CHAPTER SIX:
A Gastronomic Journey through Komodo

Embarking on a journey to Komodo is not only an exploration of its natural wonders and cultural riches but also a tantalizing adventure for the taste buds. The culinary landscape of Komodo is as diverse and captivating as its landscapes, offering a delightful array of flavors that reflect its rich history, vibrant culture, and bountiful seas. Join us as we embark on a gastronomic journey through Komodo, savoring traditional delicacies, indulging in seafood delights, relishing local flavors and street food, and immersing ourselves in unforgettable dining experiences.

Traditional Komodo Cuisine

At the heart of Komodo's culinary identity lies a tapestry of traditional dishes that have been lovingly crafted and passed down through generations. One of the most iconic dishes is "Pesa," a savory fish soup infused with aromatic spices that evoke the essence of the island. Prepared with fresh catch from the sea, Pesa encapsulates the flavors of Komodo's maritime heritage and is often enjoyed with steamed rice.

Another culinary gem is "Ikan Bakar," grilled fish marinated with a blend of spices that create a symphony of flavors. The fish is often caught locally and cooked over an open flame, infusing it with a smoky and tantalizing aroma. Accompanied by sambal, a chili-based condiment, Ikan Bakar is a testament to the harmony between local ingredients and time-honored techniques.

Seafood Delights

Komodo is a sanctuary for seafood lovers because of its close proximity to the abundant waters of the Indonesian archipelago. The seafood selections celebrate the wealth of the ocean with a variety of fish species, soft squid, and luscious prawns.

Restaurants that specialize in seafood and neighborhood eateries offer a variety of dishes that emphasize the true flavors of the ocean. A delicious balance of simplicity and indulgence may be found in grilled prawns served with aromatic rice and a squeeze of lime. A delicious crunch and burst of oceanic flavor come from well battered and fried calamari.

Local Flavors and Street Food

To truly immerse oneself in the local gastronomic scene, venturing into the realm of street food is a must. Komodo's bustling markets and food stalls offer a cornucopia of flavors that awaken the senses and transport diners into the heart of the island's culinary traditions.

The popular street meal "Kue Lumpur," a traditional cake made from glutinous rice and coconut milk, is frequently eaten as a sweet snack. It perfectly encapsulates the comfort food culture of Komodo with its gooey texture and gentle sweetness. "Babi Guling," a local variation on roasted pork, exemplifies the island's mix of tastes by fusing local spices with culinary influences from nearby regions.

Dining Experiences

Beyond the conventional and the casual, Komodo provides a variety of eating options to suit different tastes and preferences. Offering the chance to indulge in culinary masterpieces that are as aesthetically pleasing as they are savory, upscale restaurants and seaside cafes offer a fusion of international and local cuisines.

Imagine dining under the stars, with the gentle sound of the waves as your soundtrack and a plate of freshly caught seafood before you. Such experiences, often accompanied by traditional music and warm hospitality, elevate dining to an art form that engages not only the taste buds but also the heart and soul.

A culinary tour of Komodo is a celebration of tastes that capture the essence of the island—its marine history, cultural richness, and the friendliness of its inhabitants. Each taste is a journey into the heart of Komodo, from traditional dishes that honor ancestors' recipes to seafood delights that honor the ocean's generosity to street cuisine excursions that welcome culinary exploration.

Enjoying the traditional food allows you to connect with the land, the water, and the diverse array of life that makes Komodo unique while also tantalizing your taste senses. The aromas of Komodo will stay on your palate, a recall of a journey that awoke all of your senses and took you closer to the heart of this enchanting place, just as the island's landscapes left an everlasting stamp on your memories.

CHAPTER SEVEN:
Experiencing Komodo's Culture and Traditions

Beyond its stunning landscapes and diverse marine life, Komodo offers a rich tapestry of culture and traditions that captivate the heart and soul of travelers. From vibrant festivals and time-honored celebrations to intricate arts and crafts, indigenous communities, and profound rituals, Komodo's cultural heritage is a treasure trove waiting to be explored. Join us as we embark on a journey to experience Komodo's culture and traditions, immersing ourselves in the rhythms of life that have shaped this enchanting destination.

Local Festivals and Celebrations

The Komodo calendar is embellished with a tapestry of festivals and events that capture the island's rich culture and comradery. These events provide opportunities for celebration as well as glimpses into the core of Komodo culture.

The Labuan Bajo Festival, a vibrant festival that features traditional music, dancing, and art, is one of the most important events. This event, which takes place every year, is a colorful representation of the cultural richness of Komodo and a symbol of the sense of community that unites its populations.

The Sail Komodo Festival honors the region's marine heritage and takes place in conjunction with the biennial Sail Indonesia event. It highlights the island's historical and cultural ties to the sea by bringing together boats, regattas, and cultural acts.

Traditional Arts and Crafts

Komodo's indigenous arts and crafts are a beautiful way to showcase its artistic heritage. Each item is a work of love that preserves the island's cultural identity, from deft weavings and carvings to vivid textiles and pottery.

The art of ikat weaving, a technique passed down through generations, produces textiles adorned with intricate patterns and vibrant colors. These textiles not only reflect the skills of the artisans but also tell stories of myth, legend, and daily life.

The carvings on ceremonial items and traditional boats are evidence of the island's reverence for ancestral spirits and its connection to the sea. These artistic productions serve more than just aesthetic purposes; they also serve as tools of cultural transmission and historical preservation.

Indigenous Communities

The Komodo Island's native communities are in charge of maintaining long-standing customs. The island has been home to the Ata Modo ethnic group, also known as the Komodo, for many years. Their distinctive way of life, which is closely linked to the natural world and the ocean, provides a glimpse into the island's historical cultures.

As visitors engage with these communities, they gain insight into traditional fishing techniques, handcrafting skills, and age-old practices. Homestays and cultural exchanges offer opportunities to interact with the local people, fostering a deeper appreciation for their way of life and creating connections that transcend language barriers.

Rituals and Customs

Rituals and customs form the heartbeat of Komodo's culture, binding the past with the present and guiding communities through the passages of life. Adat ceremonies, traditional rituals that honor life events such as birth, marriage, and death, are a testament to the island's spiritual connection to its heritage.

Annually, the western region of Flores hosts the Pasola Festival, which features a distinct style of ritual fighting. This rite, which is based on animist ideas, is a potent illustration of the island's native spirituality and the symbiotic interaction between people and nature.

Experiencing Komodo's culture and traditions is a journey that unveils the depth of human connection to the land, the sea, and the rhythms of life. Through festivals that celebrate unity, arts and crafts that breathe life into stories, indigenous communities that embody ancestral wisdom, and rituals that honor the sacred, travelers become witnesses to the tapestry of heritage that defines Komodo.

You become a part of the story as you immerse yourself in these cultural experiences, bridging the gap between tradition and modernity and past and present. The cultural contacts and traditions you embrace become a part of your own story, deepening your journey and tying you to the core of this extraordinary place, just as the landscapes and waters of Komodo leave an indelible stamp on your memory.

CHAPTER EIGHT:
Insider's Tips for a Seamless Komodo Trip

A journey to Komodo promises a world of adventure, natural beauty, and cultural immersion. To ensure that your trip is not only memorable but also seamless, it's essential to navigate the intricacies of the destination with insight and preparation. From mastering language essentials and understanding cultural etiquette to prioritizing safety precautions and embracing sustainable travel practices, these insider's tips will empower you to make the most of your Komodo experience while leaving a positive impact on the environment and the local communities.

Language Essentials

While Bahasa Indonesia is the official language of the archipelago, English is widely spoken in tourist hubs like Labuan Bajo. Familiarizing yourself with a few basic Indonesian phrases can greatly enhance your interactions with locals and demonstrate your respect for their culture.

"Selamat pagi" (good morning), "terima kasih" (thank you), and "tolong" (please) are simple expressions that go a long way in building rapport and showing appreciation. Additionally, having a translation app handy can help bridge any language gaps and make navigation smoother.

Cultural Etiquette

Respecting local customs and traditions is paramount when engaging with Komodo's communities. In traditional villages and sacred sites, it's customary to dress modestly, covering shoulders and knees. When visiting homes or interacting with locals, removing your shoes is a sign of respect.

As a guest, it's essential to ask for permission before taking photographs, especially of individuals. Showing genuine interest in their way of life and seeking permission to capture their stories through photographs fosters positive connections and enriches your cultural experience.

Safety Precautions

Any vacation experience must put safety first, and Komodo is no different. Wear the proper footwear and equipment to avoid injury when exploring the rough terrains or participating in water sports. Given the tropical temperature, keeping hydrated and protecting yourself from the sun are other important issues.

If you're embarking on hiking or trekking excursions, it's advisable to hire a local guide who is familiar with the terrain and can ensure your safety. Pay attention to local regulations and guidelines, especially in protected areas such as the Komodo National Park, to minimize your impact on the environment.

Sustainable Travel Practices

Adopting sustainable habits is crucial for maintaining Komodo's pristine beauty for future generations as a responsible traveler. Choose eco-friendly lodgings that have an emphasis on preservation and reduce their ecological imprint. These businesses frequently use techniques like trash management, water saving, and renewable energy sources.

By bringing a reusable water bottle and cloth shopping bags, you may reduce the usage of single-use plastics. Take out your waste properly, and if there are beach clean-up programs available, take part in them. When snorkeling or diving, show respect for marine life by not touching or upsetting coral or marine life.

An insider's guide to a seamless Komodo trip encompasses more than just logistics—it's about embracing a mindset of respect, curiosity, and responsibility. By mastering language essentials, you open doors to genuine connections. Understanding cultural etiquette allows you to immerse yourself in the local way of life with grace. Prioritizing safety ensures that your adventures are not only exhilarating but also secure. Embracing sustainable travel practices lets you leave a positive mark on the environment and communities you encounter.

Ultimately, your Komodo journey is an opportunity to craft meaningful memories, both for yourself and for the destination you explore. As you traverse the landscapes, engage with the culture, and partake in thrilling experiences, your commitment to being an informed and conscientious traveler elevates your trip from a mere excursion to a transformative and impactful adventure.

CHAPTER NINE:
Komodo's Accommodation Options

As you embark on your Komodo adventure, finding the perfect place to rest and rejuvenate after a day of exploration is essential. Komodo offers a diverse range of accommodation options that cater to different preferences and budgets, ensuring that every traveler finds their ideal haven amidst this paradise of natural wonders. From luxurious resorts and boutique hotels to eco-friendly lodgings and immersive homestays, Komodo's accommodations are as diverse as the landscapes they inhabit.

Luxurious Resorts and Villas

Komodo's selection of opulent resorts and villas offers an opulent hideaway amidst the spectacular beauty of the archipelago for tourists looking for the height of luxury and comfort. These luxurious apartments create an oasis of calm and quiet by fusing lavish amenities with breath-taking views.

Sample Accommodation: AYANA Komodo Resort

The AYANA Komodo Resort, located in the center of Labuan Bajo, oozes elegance everywhere you look. This resort offers a haven of indulgence with its private beach, infinity pool, and top-notch spa. Elegant villas or lavish suites are available to guests, both of which include stunning views of the surrounding landscapes and contemporary décor.

Boutique Hotels

Intimate and individualized experiences are provided by boutique hotels in Komodo, where each little element is carefully chosen to provide an unforgettable stay. These lodgings frequently combine regional charm with contemporary comfort, creating a cozy and welcoming atmosphere that reflects the destination's cultural diversity.

Sample Accommodation: Le Pirate Island Labuan Bajo

A delightful boutique hotel that epitomizes casual elegance is Le Pirate Island Labuan Bajo. It is located on a private island and offers a range of beachfront bungalows with a unique minimalist style. Hammocks are available for guests to relax on while they enjoy fresh seafood and the ease of island life.

Eco-Friendly Accommodations

For tourists that care about the environment, Komodo has a variety of eco-friendly accommodations that respect the surroundings and place an emphasis on sustainable methods. These lodgings enable visitors to see nature up close while being mindful of the fragile ecosystems they come across.

Sample Accommodation: Seraya Resort

On Seraya Island, the Seraya Resort is a model of eco-friendly luxury. The resort runs fully on solar power and collects rainwater as part of its dedication to ecological practices. Visitors can experience off-grid living in luxurious beachside bungalows while taking advantage of diving and snorkeling in crystal-clear aquatic environments.

Homestays and Guesthouses

Homestays and guesthouses offer a genuine immersion experience for tourists looking to get to know the local people and culture. Staying with local families allows for cultural exchange and sincere relationships while providing a window into Komodo's inhabitants' daily life.

Sample Accommodation: Pondok SVD Homestay

The Pondok SVD Homestay welcomes guests with open arms in the center of Labuan Bajo. A homestay run by a local family offers cozy lodgings, a shared kitchen, and the chance to interact with the hosts. Visitors can enjoy authentic Indonesian cuisine, discover local customs, and establish connections that go beyond the norm.

Komodo's accommodation options encompass a spectrum of experiences, each catering to unique preferences and offering a distinct perspective on this captivating destination. Whether you seek the opulence of luxurious resorts, the charm of boutique hotels, the sustainability of eco-friendly lodgings, or the authenticity of homestays, Komodo ensures that your retreat is tailored to perfection.

As you traverse the landscapes and waters of this mesmerizing archipelago, your chosen accommodation becomes a haven where you recharge, reflect, and relish in the memories of your adventures. From lavish comfort to intimate charm, eco-conscious living to immersive cultural exchange, Komodo's accommodations are not just places to stay—they are integral elements of your journey, enhancing your connection with the destination and enriching your encounter with its unparalleled beauty and allure.

CHAPTER TEN:
Captivating Komodo: History and Legends

Beneath the azure skies and amidst the natural wonders of Komodo lies a rich tapestry of history and legends that have shaped the island's identity. From its maritime heritage and ancient ruins to the enchanting tales of mythical creatures and folklore, Komodo's history and legends add depth and intrigue to its captivating allure. Join us as we embark on a journey through time, uncovering the stories that have woven the fabric of Komodo's past and continue to inspire its present.

Maritime Heritage

The sea has played a significant role in Komodo's history, leaving an indelible impact on the island's identity through maritime trade and sailing expertise. Trading ships, explorers, and sailors have traveled the seas surrounding Komodo throughout history, creating a complex tapestry of cultural influences.

The "phinisi," or local traditional boats, are evidence of Komodo's nautical history. These intricately detailed wooden bowls, which have been made by experienced craftsmen for ages, have a peculiar shape. Boat building is a kind of art that symbolizes the island's relationship to the ocean as a source of inspiration, exploration, and nutrition.

Ancient Ruins and Temples

Ancient civilizations have left behind artifacts that decorate the landscapes of Komodo, providing a window into their way of life. The ruins of stone buildings and temples serve as silent witnesses to history and the tales of long-gone generations.

One such site is Batu Cermin Cave, a natural limestone cave adorned with fascinating stalactites and stalagmites. Ancient inscriptions and markings on the cave walls serve as cryptic messages from the past, inviting visitors to speculate about the hands that etched them and the purposes they served.

Mythical Stories and Folklore

The realms of myth and reality intertwine in Komodo, where mythical stories and folklore infuse the island with a sense of enchantment. Among the most captivating tales is that of Ora, the mythical sea serpent believed to inhabit the waters surrounding Komodo. Ora is both feared and revered by the local communities, representing the delicate balance between humans and the natural world.

Legends also describe the island's enigmatic beginnings. Local legend holds that the island was created when a celestial being used a miraculous sea pearl to create land. This story creates a narrative that emphasizes the island's strong ties to the natural world and the spiritual worlds.

Komodo invites us to cross the limits of time and imagination as we explore its history and stories. The island's maritime history, old ruins that reveal tales of bygone civilizations, and mythological tales that inspire awe all work together to weave a tapestry of narratives that enhance the Komodo experience.

These tales aren't just artifacts from the past; they are active strands that continue to influence how people view and interact with Komodo today. A voyage that honors the interaction between human history and the timeless forces of nature that characterize this alluring location, travelers become a part of a continuous drama as they explore the island's landscapes, interact with its residents, and immerse themselves in its cultural tapestry.

CHAPTER ELEVEN:
Beyond Komodo: Exploring Nearby Islands

While Komodo Island is a place of wonder and magic on its own, the surrounding islands' attraction tempts visitors to venture farther out. This tour enables travelers to explore the various tapestries of landscapes, cultures, and experiences that lie in these close havens, from the energetic entrance of Flores to the cultural riches of Sumba and the hidden gems of lesser-known islands.

Flores: Gateway to Komodo's Treasures

The island of Flores acts as a magical introduction to the treasures that await at the entrance to the Komodo National Park. The word "Flores" is a Portuguese word that means "flowers," which is a good description of the island's beautiful vistas covered in colorful vegetation.

Many Komodo expeditions begin in the lively town of Labuan Bajo, which is located on Flores' westernmost point. In addition to serving as a logistical hub, Labuan Bajo has a variety of other attractions to offer, such as breath-taking vistas, bustling marketplaces, and chances to experience local culture firsthand.

Traditional communities like Bena and Wae Rebo provide a window into the pre-contact way of life of the island's indigenous communities for individuals with a passion for cultural research. With its distinctive cone-shaped thatched homes hidden among the foggy mountains, Wae Rebo in particular serves as a testament to the peaceful cohabitation between humans and environment.

Sumba and its Unique Culture

A short journey from Komodo brings travelers to the island of Sumba, where a tapestry of unique traditions and cultures awaits. Sumba is renowned for its elaborate megalithic burial sites, where towering stone monuments pay homage to the island's ancestral spirits. These sites, known as "marapu," offer a glimpse into the island's spiritual beliefs and the reverence for those who have passed.

The beautiful handwoven textiles of Sumba also showcase the island's distinctive cultural identity. A centuries-old craft known as "ikat" weaving creates textiles with elaborate designs and vivid colors. Visitors may see the painstaking process of creating these pieces of art and learn about the histories, heritages, and identities represented in each piece.

The Pasola Festival, which takes place every year in Sumba, is a captivating spectacle that highlights the island's animist customs. It is thought that this ritualized type of fighting, in which horsemen hurl wooden spears at one another, will bring about abundant crops and social harmony.

Lesser-Known Islands and Destinations

Beyond the well-trodden paths lie lesser-known islands and destinations that promise unique and off-the-beaten-path experiences. The island of Alor, for instance, is a haven for divers and snorkelers, with its vibrant coral reefs, underwater gardens, and a rich marine ecosystem. Alor's welcoming communities and untouched landscapes provide a serene escape from the bustling world.

Solor and Adonara, two volcanic islands, offer a glimpse into the interplay of nature's forces. The islands are adorned with picturesque beaches, traditional villages, and the opportunity to witness the mesmerizing sight of Ile Lewotolok, an active volcano.

Rote Island, known for its relaxed atmosphere and stunning coastline, offers a tranquil retreat for those seeking respite. Its warm waters and uncrowded beaches create an idyllic setting for swimming, surfing, and enjoying the simple pleasures of island life.

Beyond the captivating realm of Komodo lies a realm of discovery that extends to nearby islands, each offering a unique facet of Indonesia's diverse cultural and natural heritage. From the gateway of Flores, where the Komodo adventure begins, to the cultural richness of Sumba and the lesser-known islands that beckon with their own enchantments, this journey transcends geographical boundaries to encompass a multi-faceted odyssey.

As travelers venture beyond Komodo's shores, they not only deepen their connection to the region's cultural tapestry but also expand their horizons, forging memories that span lush landscapes, vibrant traditions, and captivating stories. Each island, each destination, offers a chapter in the narrative of exploration—a testament to the vast and captivating tapestry of the Indonesian archipelago that continues to inspire and enthrall.

CHAPTER TWELVE:
Komodo for Adventure Seekers

Komodo, a land of untamed beauty and extraordinary biodiversity, is a paradise not only for those seeking tranquility and relaxation but also for adventure enthusiasts hungry for thrilling experiences. From traversing rugged terrains and kayaking through pristine waters to capturing wildlife through the lens and engaging in extreme outdoor activities, Komodo offers a playground where adrenaline and wonder intertwine. Join us as we delve into the heart of Komodo's adventurous spirit, exploring the myriad opportunities that beckon adventure seekers to dive headfirst into the thrill of exploration.

Trekking and Hiking Trails

The trekking and hiking trails in Komodo provide a world of adventure for those who enjoy the challenge of overcoming rocky terrain and climbing to stunning heights. With its expansive views and colorful surroundings, the famous Padar Island is a hiker's paradise. Adventuresome travelers are rewarded for their ascent to its summit with expansive vistas that span across undulating hills, blue waters, and powdery beaches—a sight that stays in the mind long after the trek is over.

The trails on Rinca Island take travelers through a variety of landscapes and provide them the opportunity to see the magnificent Komodo dragons in their natural environment. In addition to the amazing reptiles, guided excursions also highlight the island's diverse array of other animals and plants.

Kayaking and Paddleboarding

Komodo's waters are so pure that you may look down and discover the fascinating underwater environment. Adventurers can glide over vivid coral reefs when kayaking or paddleboarding, see marine life, and find undiscovered bays and lagoons.

Paddling around the calm bays of Kanawa Island offers an opportunity to immerse yourself in the serenity of nature, while kayaking through the labyrinthine passages of Rangko Cave unveils a hidden world of limestone formations and emerald waters. Whether you choose to embark on a guided tour or strike out on your own, kayaking and paddleboarding in Komodo promise moments of tranquility and awe.

Wildlife Photography

Komodo's wildlife is a living testament to the wonders of the natural world, and for photographers, it's a canvas waiting to be immortalized. From the iconic Komodo dragons to the colorful marine creatures that inhabit the coral reefs, the opportunities for capturing breathtaking shots are boundless.

To capture the dragons in their natural habitat, photography enthusiasts can embark on guided tours of Rinca Island and Komodo Island. The challenge lies in capturing the essence of these majestic creatures—their formidable presence, ancient allure, and the delicate balance they maintain within their ecosystem.

Extreme Sports and Outdoor Activities

Komodo provides a variety of extreme sports and outdoor activities that push the bounds of adventure for those looking for the ultimate surge of excitement. Divers and snorkelers can descend into the marine paradise of Komodo National Park, where encounters with manta rays, sharks, and vivid coral formations are the stuff of legends.

Rock climbers can test their prowess on the cliffs of Batu Cermin Cave and Gili Lawa Darat, all while taking in the gorgeous scenery. The difficulty transforms into a dance with nature's forces as you negotiate the rugged terrain, rewarding your efforts with breath-taking views.

Beyond its stunning beaches and vibrant coral reefs, Komodo is enticing to adventurers who wish to test their limitations, embrace the uncharted, and savor the thrill of discovery. Komodo's playground gives an opportunity to experience the planet in its most unadulterated, exhilarating form, whether you're walking through harsh terrains, kayaking through secret coves, photographing wildlife, or taking part in extreme sports against breathtaking backgrounds.

As you go out on these perilous adventures, you not only put your mettle to the test but also develop a close bond with nature. An adventurer's voyage that indelibly imprints your spirit, the heart-pounding moments, the spectacular landscapes, and the palpable sense of wonder that come with each adventure become everlasting memories and weave themselves into the tapestry of your Komodo journey.

CHAPTER THIRTEEN: Appendix

As you embark on your Komodo adventure, a well-prepared journey is key to ensuring a seamless and enriching experience. In this comprehensive appendix, we provide you with essential tools and resources that will enhance your trip and help you navigate the nuances of travel in this captivating destination.

30 Useful Phrases in Local Language with pronunciation guide

Familiarizing yourself with basic phrases in the local language can go a long way in enhancing your interactions and connecting with the local communities. Here are 30 useful phrases in Bahasa Indonesia:

1. Selamat pagi (seh-lah-maht pah-gee) - Good morning.

2. Terima kasih (teh-ree-mah kah-see) - Thank you.

3. Tolong (toh-long) - Please.

4. Apa kabar? (ah-pah kah-bar) - How are you?

5. Permisi (pehr-mee-see) - Excuse me.

6. Saya tidak tahu (sah-yah tee-dahk tah-hoo) - I don't know.

7. Nama saya... (nah-mah sah-yah) - My name is...

8. Di mana toilet? (dee mah-nah toy-let) - Where is the toilet?

9. Boleh bicara bahasa Inggris? (boh-leh bee-chah-rah bah-hah-sah Ing-gris) - Can you speak English?

10. Berapa harganya? (beh-rah-pah hahr-gah-nya) - How much does it cost?

11. Tidak apa-apa (tee-dahk ah-pah-ah-pah) - It's okay.

12. Tolong bantu saya (toh-long ban-too sah-yah) - Please help me.

13. Maaf (mah-ahf) - Sorry.

14. Ya (yah) - Yes.

15. Tidak (tee-dahk) - No.

16. Saya lapar (sah-yah lah-pahr) - I'm hungry.

17. Saya haus (sah-yah hah-oos) - I'm thirsty.

18. Baik (bah-eek) - Good.

19. Tidak baik (tee-dahk bah-eek) - Not good.

20. Di sini (dee see-nee) - Here.

21. Di sana (dee sah-nah) - There.

22. Bagaimana? (bah-gai-mah-nah) - How?

23. Dimana? (dee-mah-nah) - Where?

24. Kapan? (kah-pahn) - When?

25. Siapa? (see-ah-pah) - Who?

26. Kenapa? (keh-nah-pah) - Why?

27. Bagus (bah-goos) - Good/nice.

28. Tidak apa-apa (tee-dahk ah-pah-ah-pah) - It's okay.

29. Selamat tinggal (seh-lah-maht teeng-gahl) - Goodbye.

30. Sampai jumpa (sahm-pie joohm-pah) - See you later.

Currency Conversion Guide

Understanding the local currency and its value in your home currency is crucial for budgeting and making informed financial decisions. The currency used in Indonesia is the Indonesian Rupiah (IDR). To convert your currency to IDR, you can use online currency conversion tools or mobile apps.

Here are some sample currency conversions from Indonesian Rupiah (IDR) to several major world currencies as of the current date. Please keep in mind that exchange rates can fluctuate frequently, so these values may change over time. For the most up-to-date rates, it's recommended to check with a reliable financial source or currency converter.

1. Indonesian Rupiah to United States Dollar (USD):
  - 10,000 IDR = Approximately 0.70 USD
  - 50,000 IDR = Approximately 3.50 USD
  - 100,000 IDR = Approximately 7.00 USD
  - 500,000 IDR = Approximately 35.00 USD
  - 1,000,000 IDR = Approximately 70.00 USD

2. Indonesian Rupiah to Euro (EUR):
  - 10,000 IDR = Approximately 0.59 EUR
  - 50,000 IDR = Approximately 2.95 EUR
  - 100,000 IDR = Approximately 5.90 EUR

- 500,000 IDR = Approximately 29.50 EUR

- 1,000,000 IDR = Approximately 59.00 EUR

3. Indonesian Rupiah to British Pound (GBP):

- 10,000 IDR = Approximately 0.51 GBP

- 50,000 IDR = Approximately 2.57 GBP

- 100,000 IDR = Approximately 5.15 GBP

- 500,000 IDR = Approximately 25.75 GBP

- 1,000,000 IDR = Approximately 51.50 GBP

4. Indonesian Rupiah to Australian Dollar (AUD):

- 10,000 IDR = Approximately 0.97 AUD

- 50,000 IDR = Approximately 4.85 AUD

- 100,000 IDR = Approximately 9.70 AUD

- 500,000 IDR = Approximately 48.50 AUD

- 1,000,000 IDR = Approximately 97.00 AUD

Please note that these are approximate conversions and may vary slightly based on the source and current market conditions. It's always a good idea to check with a reliable currency converter or financial institution for the most accurate and up-to-date exchange rates before making any currency-related transactions.

Packing Checklist

A well-organized packing list ensures that you have all the essentials you need for a comfortable and enjoyable journey. Here's a comprehensive packing checklist tailored to your Komodo adventure:

1. Clothing:

- Lightweight and breathable clothing for the tropical climate

- Swimsuits and cover-ups for beach activities

- Comfortable walking shoes for hiking and exploring

- Sun protection gear: hats, sunglasses, sunscreen, and UPF clothing

- Rain jacket or poncho, especially during the wet season

- Long-sleeved clothing for sun protection and mosquito prevention

2. Travel Essentials:

- Passport, visa, and any necessary travel documents

- Travel insurance and copies of important documents

- Prescribed medications and a basic first aid kit

- Power adapters for local electrical outlets

- Reusable water bottle and water purification tablets

- Camera and photography equipment

3. Outdoor Gear:

- Snorkeling or diving equipment if you have your own

- Sturdy daypack for hiking and exploring

- Insect repellent and mosquito nets if camping

4. Miscellaneous:

- Cash in local currency (Indonesian Rupiah) and small denominations

- Toiletries and personal hygiene items

- Ziplock bags for storing wet items and protecting valuables

- Local SIM card for mobile data (optional)

Emergency Contacts

While Komodo offers a breathtaking adventure, it's essential to be prepared for any unexpected situations. Make note of the following emergency contacts:

1. Emergency Services: 112
2. Medical Assistance: Local hospital/clinic contact information
3. Police: 110
4. Tourist Police: Contact details of the nearest tourist police office

Additionally, keep a copy of your travel insurance policy and emergency contacts in a safe and easily accessible place.

This comprehensive appendix serves as your ultimate companion, equipping you with the tools and resources needed to make the most of your Komodo adventure. From a meticulously curated packing checklist to useful phrases in the local language, currency conversion guidance, and emergency contacts, this guide ensures that you're well-prepared, connected, and informed as you explore the wonders of Komodo and its neighboring islands. With this appendix by your side, you can embark on your journey with confidence, curiosity, and a spirit of adventure that knows no bounds.

MAP OF KOMODO

Komodo National Park

Made in United States
Troutdale, OR
12/10/2023